Scary Snakes

Boas

PowerKiDS
press
New York

Julie Fiedler

Published in 2008 by The Rosen Publishing Group, Inc.
29 East 21st Street, New York, NY 10010

First Edition

Editor: Jennifer Way
Book Design: Julio Gil
Layout Design: Kate Laczynski
Photo Researcher: Nicole Pristash

Photo Credits: Cover, pp. 1, 7, 11 (main), 13, 17 © Shutterstock.com; p. 5, 15 © www.istockphoto.com/ Brasil 2; p. 9 by Erica Clendening; p. 11 (inset), 19, 21 © Wolfgang Wuster.

Library of Congress Cataloging-in-Publication Data

Fiedler, Julie.
  Boas / Julie Fiedler. — 1st ed.
      p. cm. — (Scary snakes)
  Includes index.
  ISBN-13: 978-1-4042-3836-7 (library binding)
  ISBN-10: 1-4042-3836-0 (library binding)
  1. Boidae—Juvenile literature. I. Title.
  QL666.O63F54 2008
  597.96'7—dc22
                                    2007006488

Manufactured in the United States of America

Contents

What Are Boas?

Different types of snakes belong to different groups called families. Boas belong to the family of snakes called Boidae. They are a lot like pythons because both types of snakes are **constrictors**.

Most kinds of boas have a large head and mouth. Different kinds of boas have different patterns, or markings, along their back. Female boas are generally bigger than males. Boas do not have **venomous** bites, like some snakes do, but do not be fooled. They are still very **dangerous**.

Several kinds of boas live in the trees of South America's rain forests. The boa shown here lives in Brazil.

A Tight Squeeze

Boas kill **prey** by **squeezing** it to death. When boas squeeze, they do not break their prey's bones. They kill by constricting their prey.

Constriction works when boas capture prey and **coil** their body around them. Then they use their powerful muscles to squeeze their body tighter and tighter. When the prey cannot breathe anymore, it dies. This kind of death is called **suffocation**. Anacondas can kill prey as big as a deer!

When a boa constricts its prey, the prey dies because it cannot breathe. Each time the prey breathes out, the boa squeezes tighter. It will keep doing this until the prey dies.

Boas on the Hunt

When boas hunt, they capture prey by biting, or striking, quickly. Then they coil around the prey and start constricting.

Once boas kill prey, they open their jaws, or mouthparts, very wide. They swallow their prey whole starting with its head. Boas can open their mouth wider than other snakes and can eat animals that are bigger than their jaws. It can take boas days to **digest** prey. If a boa eats a large animal, it can even take weeks to digest it!

This red-tailed boa is eating a rat. After eating a large meal, boas need to rest and move as little as possible. This helps them digest their meal properly.

9

Where Boas Live

Boas live all over the world except for Australia. Boas live in many different **habitats**, such as rain forests, grasslands, and deserts. Some boas are **arboreal**, meaning that they live in trees. Some boas are **aquatic**, which means that they live in water. Many boas live on land in underground holes, called burrows.

Boas often live in **tropical** areas, which are warm year-round. Boas are **cold blooded** and cannot control their body temperature, or heat. Their bodily functions go faster or slower depending on if the air around them is warm or cool. This means it is easier for them to live in warmer habitats.

Boas can be found in the tropical rain forests along South America's Amazon River. The green anaconda (inset) lives in this type of habitat.

Boas on Branches

Arboreal boas, such as emerald tree boas, have a strong tail that helps them hold on to branches. An arboreal boa's tail is so strong that the snake can hang down and strike at passing prey without letting go. Arboreal boas have longer fangs, or teeth, than other boas and use them to reach out and bite their prey.

Arboreal boas have a large head and thinner body than most other kinds of boas. Their long, thin body helps them move around easily in trees. They are nocturnal, which means that they hunt at night. They have lips that sense heat, which they use to find prey in the dark.

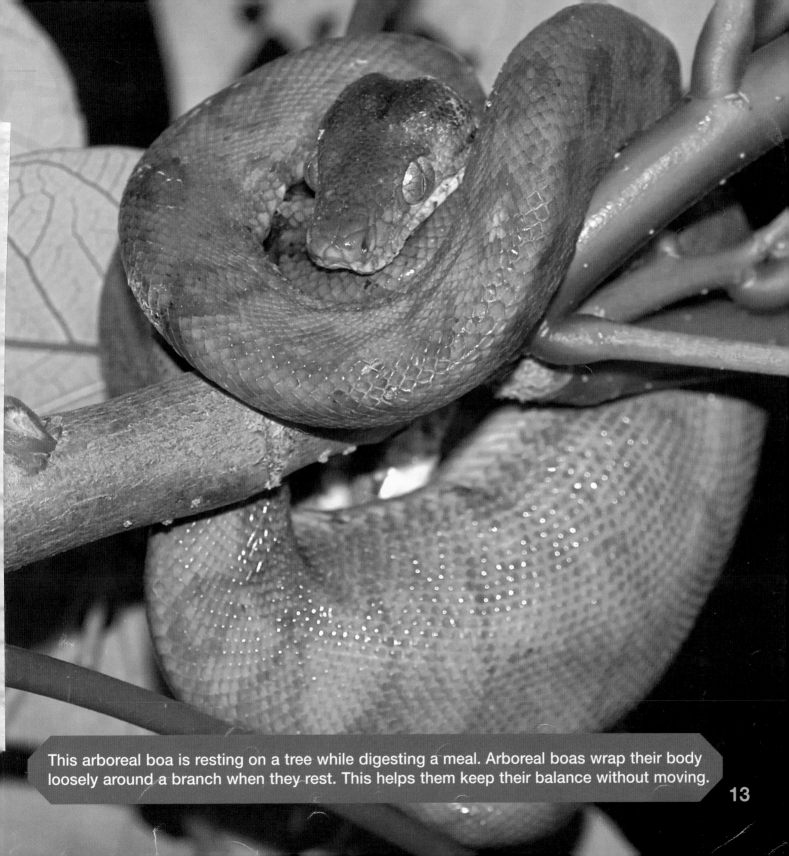

This arboreal boa is resting on a tree while digesting a meal. Arboreal boas wrap their body loosely around a branch when they rest. This helps them keep their balance without moving.

13

Young Boas

Male and female boas generally **mate** between December and March. They have bumps, called spurs, near their tail that they use during mating. Most snakes lay eggs, but female boas give birth to young that have grown inside them. They can give birth to up to 50 babies at a time!

Baby boas can be 18 inches (46 cm) long. As they grow, they shed their skin. Boas become adults in three to five years. Not all young boas live to become adults, though. Young boas have more **predators** than adult boas. Large cats, birds, and even crabs all prey on young boas.

This baby boa is small enough to fit in a person's hand. The boa will shed its skin many times as it grows into adult size, which is about eight times the size it is in this picture.

Emerald Tree Boas

Emerald tree boas live in the tropical areas of South America, such as near the Amazon River in Brazil. They are arboreal and eat birds, lizards, and small animals. They are nocturnal, like other arboreal boas.

Adults are bright green and have white stripes. The adults' coloring helps hide them among the branches and leaves in which emerald tree boas live. Babies are born bright yellow, red, or orange but turn green during their first year of life. They can grow to be 6½ feet (2 m) long and can live to be 10 to 15 years old.

The bright green emerald tree boa eats less often than boas that live on the ground. It often goes two months without eating!

Green Anacondas

Anacondas are some of the biggest snakes in the world. They can grow to be 30 feet (9 m) long and weigh more than 550 pounds (250 kg)! These thick snakes can be up to 6½ feet (2 m) around.

Green anacondas are aquatic and live in South America. They are dark green, with black marks on their back. They have eyes and nostrils on the top of their head, instead of on the side of their head, like other snakes. This helps anacondas see and breathe while they are in the water. Anacondas often kill their prey by pulling it into the water and drowning it.

You can see that the eyes and nose of the green anaconda are nearer the top of its head than on other boas. This huge aquatic snake can take down prey as large as a crocodile!

Boa Constrictors

Boa constrictors are one of the most well-known boas. They live in Central America and South America. They are light brown or cream colored and have dark brown areas on their back. Boa constrictors can climb trees, but mostly they stay on land. They often live in holes dug by other animals.

Boa constrictors can grow to be 6½ to 10 feet (2–3 m) long. One boa constrictor was found that was 18½ feet (6 m) long. They can live to be 40 years old. They eat birds, lizards, and even monkeys!

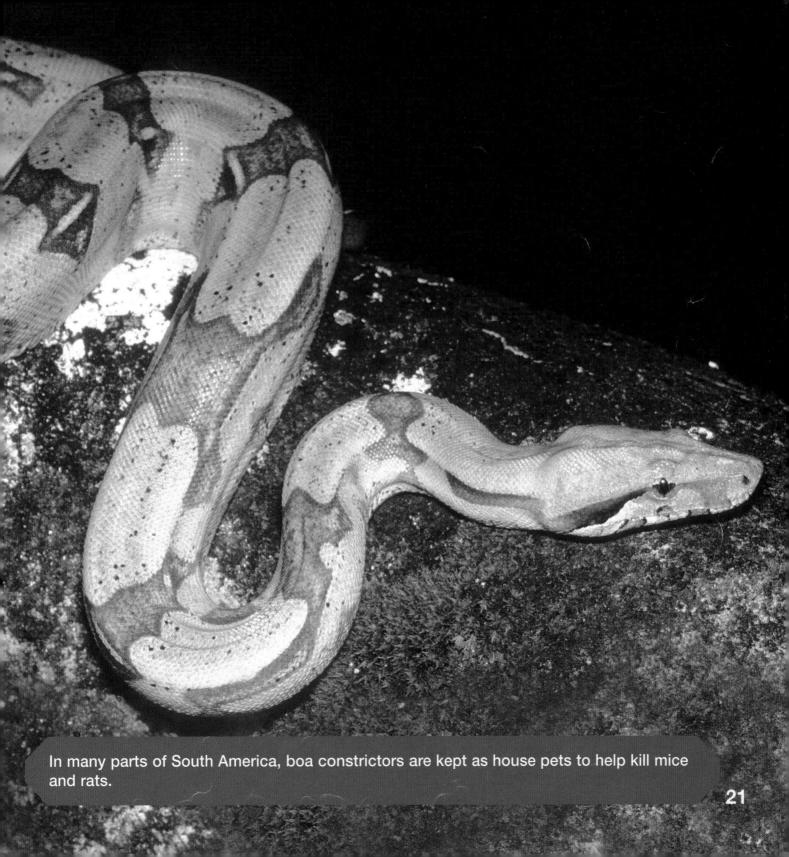

In many parts of South America, boa constrictors are kept as house pets to help kill mice and rats.

Boas and People

Boas are dangerous snakes, but people can be dangerous to boas, too! Some people hunt boas and use their skin for leather. Other people hunt boas to eat their meat. Because people kill a lot of boas, some kinds, such as Dumeril's boa, are **endangered**. Some countries make laws that do not allow people to hunt boas. These laws help keep boas safe from people.

Some people also buy boas to keep as pets. Only people who know a lot about handling snakes should do this because boas need special care and can be dangerous.

Glossary

aquatic (uh-KWAH-tik) Living or growing in water.

arboreal (ahr-BOR-ee-ul) Having to do with trees.

coil (KOYL) To curl up.

cold blooded (KOHLD BLUH-did) Having body heat that changes with the heat around the body.

constrictors (kun-STRIKT-urz) Snakes that kill by wrapping their body around their prey and squeezing.

dangerous (DAYN-jeh-rus) Might cause hurt.

digest (dy-JEST) To break down food so that the body can use it.

endangered (in-DAYN-jerd) In danger of no longer existing.

habitats (HA-beh-tats) The kinds of land where an animal or a plant naturally lives.

mate (MAYT) To come together to make babies.

predators (PREH-duh-terz) Animals that kill other animals for food.

prey (PRAY) An animal that is hunted by another animal for food.

squeezing (SKWEEZ-ing) Forcing together.

suffocation (SUH-fuh-kay-shun) When a person or an animal dies from lack of air.

tropical (TRAH-puh-kul) Warm year-round.

venomous (VEH-nuh-mis) Having a poisonous bite.

Index

B
bites, 4
body temperature, 10

C
constriction, 6
constrictors, 4, 20

D
days, 8

death, 6
December, 14
Dumeril's boa, 20

H
habitats, 10

P
predators, 14
prey, 6, 8, 12, 18

S
suffocation, 6

T
trees, 10, 12, 20
tropical areas, 10, 16

W
water, 10, 18

Web Sites

Due to the changing nature of Internet links, PowerKids Press has developed an online list of Web sites related to the subject of this book. This site is updated regularly. Please use this link to access the list:

www.powerkidslinks.com/ssn/boa/